Growth of Pioneers and Technological Advances

Heather E. Schwartz

Consultants

Dorothy Levin, M.S. Ed., MBA
St. Lucie County Schools

Vanessa Ann Gunther, Ph.D.
Department of History
Chapman University

Cassandra Slone
Pinellas County Public Schools

Publishing Credits

Rachelle Cracchiolo, M.S.Ed., *Publisher*
Conni Medina, M.A.Ed., *Managing Editor*
Emily R. Smith, M.A.Ed., *Series Developer*
Diana Kenney, M.A.Ed., NBCT, *Content Director*
Courtney Patterson, *Multimedia Designer*

Image Credits: Cover and pp.1, 2-3, 9, 13, 17 (front and back), 20-21, 21, 22-23, 23, 24, 24-25, 25, 26-27, 27, 29, 32 State Archives of Florida; pp.4-5 LOC [g3300.ct000174]; pp.4, 5, 7, 10-11, 12-13, 13, 18, 28-29, 29 North Wind Picture Archives; p.6 (right) LOC [LC-USZ62-117120], (left) LOC [LC-USZ62-104958]; p.11 State Archives of Florida/Remington; pp.14-15, 29 LOC [LC-DIG-ppmsca-18216]; p.15 LOC [LC-DIG-det-4a03545]; p.19 LOC [g3930.rr001930]; pp.20, 31 NARA [528542]; p.27 and back cover Baker Old Class Collection, Baker Library Historical Collections; all other images from iStock and/or Shutterstock.

Library of Congress Cataloging-in-Publication Data

Names: Schwartz, Heather E., author.
Title: Growth of Florida : pioneers and technological advances / Heather E.
  Schwartz.
Description: Huntington Beach, CA : Teacher Created Materials, [2017] |
  Includes index.
Identifiers: LCCN 2016014352 (print) | LCCN 2016015181 (ebook) | ISBN
  9781493835386 (pbk.) | ISBN 9781480753488 (eBook)
Subjects: LCSH: Florida--History--Juvenile literature. |
  Florida--Population--Juvenile literature. | Florida--Economic
  conditions--Juvenile literature.
Classification: LCC F311.3 .S39 2017 (print) | LCC F311.3 (ebook) | DDC
  975.9--dc23
LC record available at https://lccn.loc.gov/2016014352

Teacher Created Materials

5301 Oceanus Drive
Huntington Beach, CA 92649-1030
http://www.tcmpub.com
ISBN 978-1-4938-3538-6
© 2017 Teacher Created Materials, Inc.

Table of Contents

Change in Florida 4
Settling Florida 6
Early Industry 10
New Modes of Transportation 14
Tourists Flood In 20
Florida's Future Growth 26
Create It! 28
Glossary 30
Index 31
Your Turn! 32

Change in Florida

Florida did not always belong to the United States. The land belonged to American Indian tribes long before it became a state. As time went by, the Spanish, French, and British explored the land. They came to the New World looking to expand their empires. The land changed hands many times. It was under Spanish and British rule before it became a U.S. territory in 1819.

In the 1800s, many people moved to Florida. New business started to take shape with the influx of new people. Florida went through many changes. It became a place known for its cotton, cattle, and oranges. Business grew. The number of people in the state grew. But what exactly spurred this rapid growth?

American Indians in Florida in the 1600s

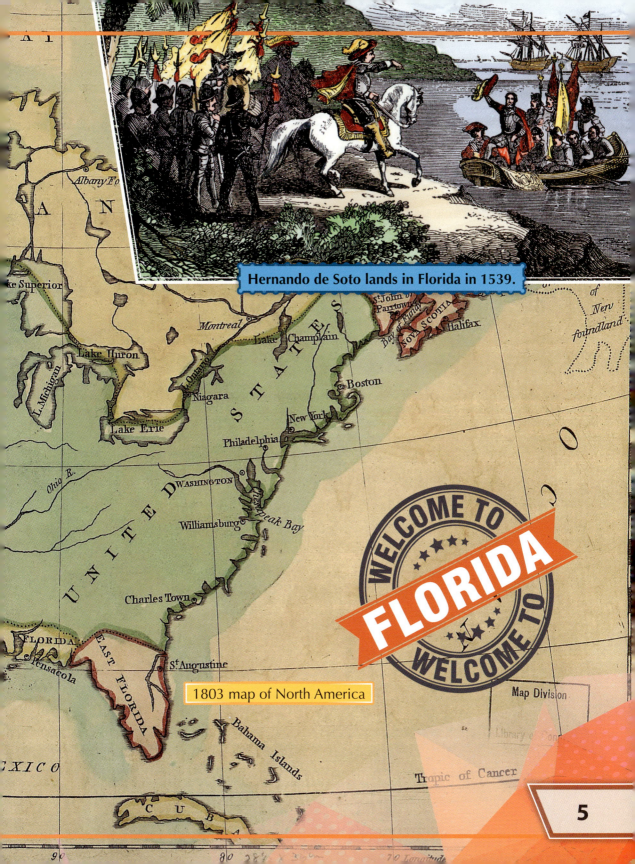

Hernando de Soto lands in Florida in 1539.

1803 map of North America

Settling Florida

American Indians were the first people to live in Florida. They were there for thousands of years. Then, Spanish and French explorers arrived in the 1500s. Spain ruled Florida for more than 200 years. Rule switched to British hands in 1763. Then, the Spanish regained control in 1783.

Florida became a U.S. territory in 1819. James Monroe was the U.S. president at the time. He asked Andrew Jackson to help him set up a **government**. Jackson agreed. He worked as the state's temporary **governor**.

In 1822, William P. Duval took over as governor. As people moved into the territory, they realized that the area was wild. It was dangerous. But **pioneers** came in spite of the risks. They moved from other parts of the country. Most came to buy land. Some thought the warm weather would be good for their health. Others were simply looking for a change from the lives they lived.

7th U.S. President

Andrew Jackson became the president of the United States in 1829.

James Monroe

Andrew Jackson

U.S. Territories

Spanish Territories

U.S. States

The Adams-Onís Treaty

In 1817, President Monroe asked Jackson to stop American Indian attacks at the Georgia-Florida border. Instead, Jackson invaded Florida. The United States won the First Seminole War in 1818. In the Adams-Onís Treaty, Spain agreed to give Florida to the United States.

territory won from Spain

British troops attack the Spanish.

Life was not easy for the early pioneers. They dealt with mosquitos and alligators. There were no roads. There were no post offices. People who chose to live in Florida were isolated.

Many people chose to live on Florida's **coast**. They relied on what they found in the water. They ate fish, shellfish, and turtles. They had to quickly learn what American Indians in the area had known for years. They had to learn which plants were edible. They had to learn how to farm the land.

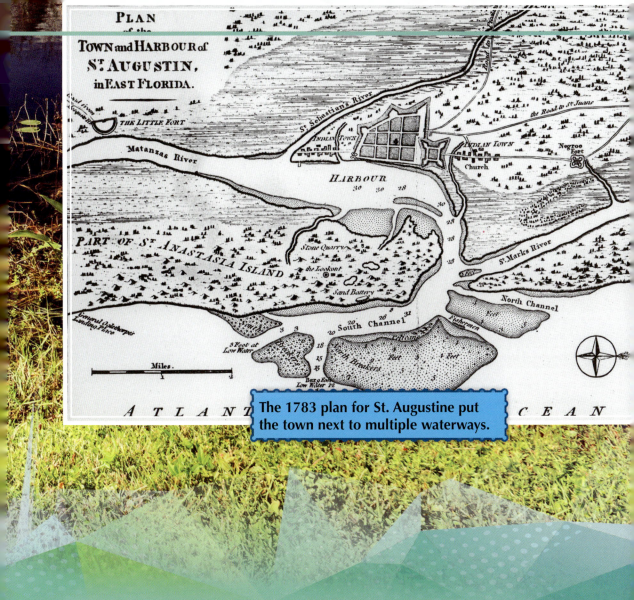

The 1783 plan for St. Augustine put the town next to multiple waterways.

People living on the coast sometimes received supplies from ships. Ships docked in Key West, Pensacola, and St. Augustine. They brought supplies and people to the state.

Some settlers lived on inland rivers. Keelboats, barges, and canoes were used to transport supplies across those shallow waters.

Early Industry

Many early settlers raised cattle. The Spanish and the British first brought the cattle to Florida. It's said that some of the cattle escaped. They lived in wild herds for many years. Living in the wild made the cattle strong. They adapted to the warm **climate** over the years. They built up **immunities** to local diseases.

Florida cowmen were also strong. They kept their cattle alive through harsh weather. They protected them from threats, such as panthers and wolves. They stayed alert at all times to stop **cattle rustlers** from stealing their livestock.

Cowmen spent endless hours on cattle **drives**, moving herds from place to place. Their end goal was to bring cattle to market. But the markets were far away. Driving cattle from Florida to places as far north as South Carolina increased the risk. Cattle could die or get injured. Cowmen ran those same risks. And every animal that died reduced the money the cowmen made.

Other Names

Florida cowmen cracked their whips to control their cattle. For this reason, they were also called Crackers. Today, the term often has a negative **connotation**.

Cowmen herd cattle.

Many of Florida's early settlers were also planters. Some grew **citrus** trees near rivers. They sold the fruit to northern states. They packed it in barrels and shipped it by boat.

Other planters grew cotton on large **plantations**. Cotton grew well in the state's soil. Most cotton planters lived between the Apalachicola (ap-uh-lach-ih-KOH-luh) and Suwannee rivers.

Planters knew that new inventions could make them more **profitable**. Eli Whitney **patented** the cotton gin in 1794. The cotton gin made it easy to clean raw cotton. It separated seeds from the cotton. This increased the work that could be done in a given amount of time. But there was a catch. Planters had to pay people to harvest cotton and run the cotton gins. They still were not making as much money as they wanted. So, they bought slaves to do the work. Planters did not pay slaves. They forced them to work endless hours in poor conditions.

Eli Whitney

Eli Whitney

As a young boy, Eli Whitney loved to take things apart and put them back together. As he grew older, he saw how much trouble people had removing seeds from cotton. So, he invented a faster way to do it.

1842 advertisement selling slaves

New Modes of Transportation

The first steamboat arrived in Florida in 1827. It was powered by steam and used a paddle wheel to move. Steamboats could travel farther than standard sailing ships. They could travel inland. They could travel up narrow and winding rivers. They could reach settlers who were once isolated. They brought people to areas that had not yet been explored. They sparked people's sense of adventure.

A steamboat makes its way down the Ocklawaha River in 1902.

The influx of steamboats had a positive impact on the state. The boats made shipping easier for farmers. They could ship to more customers than ever before. This meant more money for the citrus industry. And, most of the boats carried **cargo** on their lower decks. This opened up places for people to sit on the upper decks. People and goods could travel at the same time.

People hunt alligators in 1880.

In 1834, people began to build Florida's first railroad. The rail stretched 22 miles (35 kilometers) from Tallahassee to Port Leon. The railroad wasn't what we are used to today. Mules pulled carts filled with cotton along the tracks. When they reached the port, the cotton was transferred from the carts to the ships. The ships then took the cotton where it needed to go.

Steam trains came to Florida's railroad system in 1836. The steam train is what comes to mind when most people think of railroads. The first line started in St. Joseph. It ended 9 miles (14 kilometers) down the way at the Apalachicola River. It was faster than the mules and carts had been. Another line started the next year. It connected Tallahassee to the St. Marks River.

Security in Salt

Refrigeration did not exist on trains in the early 1800s. Salt was used to preserve beef during long train rides. Luckily, Florida had access to a lot of salt in the surrounding seas.

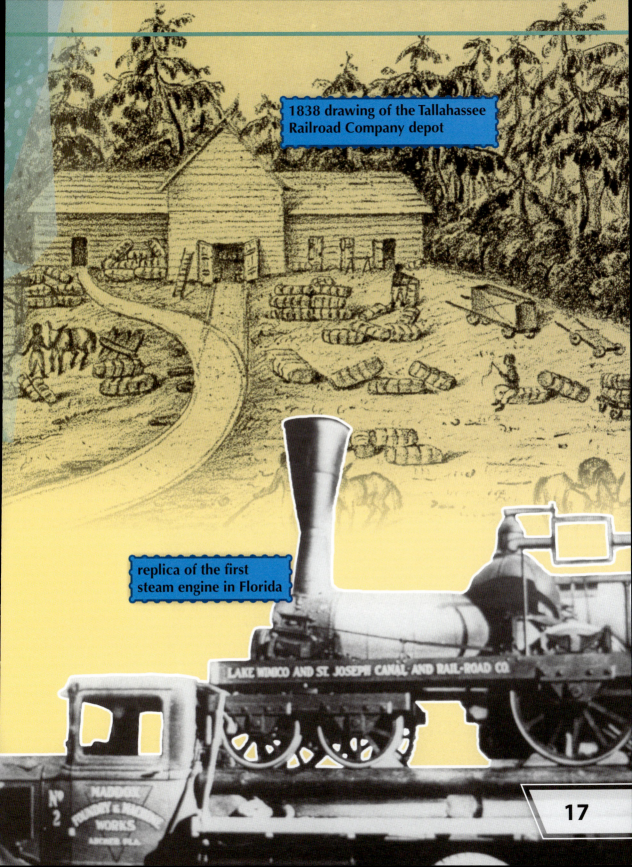

1838 drawing of the Tallahassee Railroad Company depot

replica of the first steam engine in Florida

With the advent of the steam train, businessmen started to see dollar signs. They saw a chance to make quite a bit of money moving goods and people around Florida. The only thing standing in the way was the lack of routes. But, routes could be built! Soon, railroads slowly started to appear around Florida. The Pensacola and Georgia Railroad ran from Tallahassee to Pensacola. Most of its new routes were short. Quite often, goods were shipped just as slowly as though pulled by mule-drawn carts. Train accommodations weren't enticing to passengers, either. Still, they moved goods where they needed to go. And the improved access to remote places convinced more people to move to Florida.

Florida quickly grew during this time. People had more reasons to move there. Some people moved to become farmers. Some moved to become merchants or cowmen. Others found work as craftsmen or **blacksmiths**.

blacksmiths

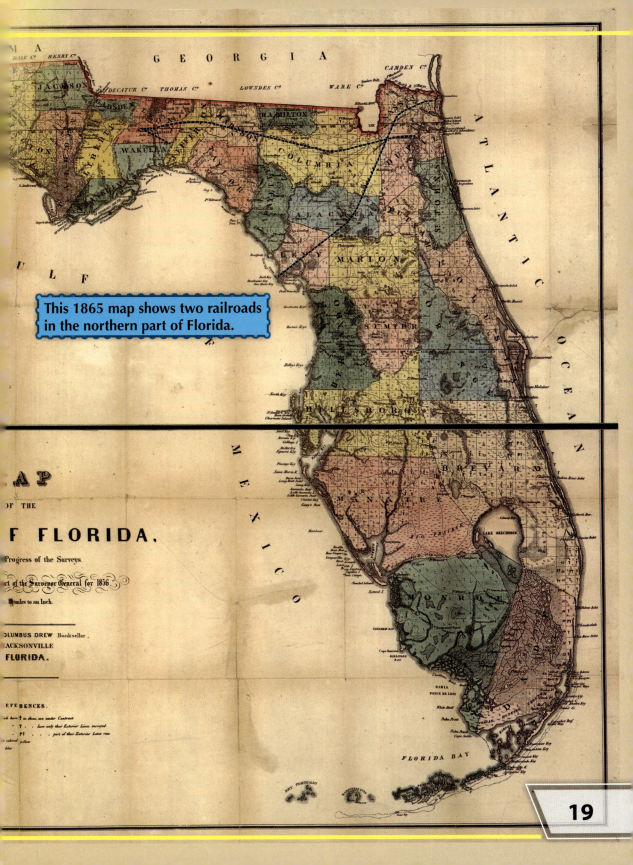

This 1865 map shows two railroads in the northern part of Florida.

Tourists Flood In

Many people were eager to move to Florida. Still, others were happy simply stopping by. They wanted to travel. They had money to spend. The **tourism** industry really started to grow after Florida became a state in 1845.

Many tourists went to Florida by steamboat. Tourists liked steamboats more than trains. Train routes were limited. The benches in the cars were hard and the tracks were bumpy. Jacob Brock saw the chance to give tourists what they wanted. He started the Brock Line in 1852. It was a steamboat line that had a set schedule for travel. Brock ran his boats along the St. Johns River. He built a hotel near there, too. He called it the Brock House. It quickly became a popular hotel and health spa.

But railroads also started to improve during this time. Senator David Yulee and other leaders got state money to increase rail expansion across the state. They wanted to connect East and West Florida.

Father of Florida Railroads

David Yulee is considered the Father of Florida Railroads. He was elected Florida's first U.S. Senator in 1845. He founded the Florida Railroad Company in 1853.

Brock House advertisement from the 1800s

More railroads started to be built across the state in the 1850s. But building came to a halt with the start of the **Civil War**. Money was needed for the war effort. Manpower was also needed. Many of the tracks were destroyed in battle—often on purpose. It was harder for the enemy to get supplies without railroads. When the war ended, owners did not have money to fix the rails.

Then, a man named Henry Plant started buying up bankrupt railroads. He founded the Plant System of railroads and steamboats in the 1880s. His system ran 2,235 miles (3,597 kilometers) from Tampa to New York. It helped people travel farther. It decreased the time it took farmers to move their goods. It also enticed cigar factory owners to open plants in Tampa. Tampa had better access to clean water than Key West. It also had easier access to ports. This location made it cheaper for the factories to import tobacco.

A Plant System train travels through Clearwater, Florida.

Bursting with People

Between 1830 and 1860, Florida's population more than quadrupled. It went from 34,730 to 140,424 people!

But, Plant didn't stop there. He opened hotels to attract tourists, too. His main hotel was the Tampa Bay Hotel. It offered the top in luxury at the time. All of the rooms had electricity. And most even had their own baths! Plant built other hotels along his train routes, too. People started to move farther south into the state.

As Plant built his system, Henry Flagler built railroads that ran as far south as present-day Miami. Flagler had ideas similar to Plant's. He thought that a lack of railroads and hotels were the only things holding the state back.

Flagler's lavish hotels were an instant success. The Hotel Ponce de León (PONS day lay-OWN) boasted more than 80 works of fine art. It was also the first large building in the country to be made of concrete.

Flagler's railroads weren't shabby either. They opened up shipping for citrus growers. They also reignited the sugar industry. Flagler even built the Overseas Railroad to Key West in 1912. He is often credited with Florida's fast population growth. His railroads helped build Florida's modern **economy**.

advertisement for the Tampa Bay Hotel

The Hotel Ponce de León was built by Henry Flagler in 1888.

Flagler City?

In 1896, Flagler helped build a city by Biscayne Bay. He financed the town's first newspaper, dug a channel, and built streets. His railroad had brought in many of the new residents. The people wanted to name the city after him. But he convinced them to name it after the nearby river—Miami.

Miami in 1896

Florida's Future Growth

Florida changed over the course of many years. It went from life under Spanish and British rule to life as a U.S. territory. It was not long until it became a state. New inventions often spurred the state's growth. Steamboats and railroads played a big role in growing the state's economy. Goods were shipped faster. People got where they needed to go. Tourists traveled to see what the state had to offer. Hotels gave them nice places to stay.

But growth didn't stop at the turn of the century. By 1920, Florida had another growth spurt. People from across the country flocked to the state to buy cheap land quickly. Almost 300,000 people moved to the state during the land **boom**.

Regardless of change, the people of the state were strong. They were pioneers. They kept evolving their state. They kept growing as part of the nation. Florida continued to work toward the future.

A crowd gathers outside of a new Florida land development in 1926.

WWI

World War I took place between 1914 and 1918. During that time, Florida served as a training ground for much of the nation's military. This increased the number of people moving into the state.

U.S. Marines learn to fly in Miami in 1918.

1925 weekly real estate guide

Create It!

Early pioneers had many new experiences when they moved to Florida. They met new people. They ate new foods. They found new jobs working with cattle and growing cotton and oranges. They also watched the world change. They saw steamboats and trains in action. They saw the country divided during the Civil War. Some even saw the states come together again.

Create a book about a pioneer's experiences. Draw pictures or find photos on the Internet. Cut them out and glue them onto paper. Write captions for the pictures. Describe how the pictures show what people experienced. Make a title page. Then, staple the pages together to make a book.

29

Glossary

blacksmiths—people who make and repair things made of iron by hand

boom—a period of growth, progress, or sudden expansion

cargo—goods that are carried from one place to another on a ship, aircraft, or motor vehicle

cattle rustlers—people who steal animals, such as cattle, horses, or sheep, from a farm or ranch

citrus—a juicy fruit that has a thick skin that grows in warm areas

Civil War—the war fought between the Northern and Southern states over the issues of slavery and state rights

climate—the usual weather conditions a place gets

coast—the land near a sea or ocean

connotation—an idea or feeling that a word makes you think about in addition to its meaning

drives—acts of leading cattle over land in a group

economy—the system of buying and selling goods and services

government—a group of leaders who make choices for a country, state, or city

governor—a person who is the leader of a region

immunities—the body's ability to fight off infections from diseases

patented—obtained a document that gave a person or company the right to be the only one that made or sold a certain product

pioneers—people who are the first to explore and settle a new place

plantations—large farms that produce crops for money

profitable—making a financial gain

tourism—the activity of traveling to a place for pleasure

Index

American Indian, 4, 6–8
cattle, 4, 10–11, 28
Civil War, 22, 28
cotton, 4, 12–13, 16, 28
cowmen, 10–11, 18
Crackers, 11
Flagler, Henry 24–25
oranges, 4, 28
pioneers, 6, 8, 26, 28
Plant, Henry, 22, 24
railroad, 16–20, 22, 24–26
ships, 9, 12, 14–16, 18, 24, 26
slaves, 12–13
Spanish, 4, 6–7, 10, 26
steamboat, 14–15, 20, 22, 26, 28
steam trains, 16–18, 28
tourism, 20
Whitney, Eli, 12–13
Yulee, David, 20

Your Turn!

Hotel Advertisement

Create an advertisement to attract visitors to a hotel you would like to open in Florida now. Where will it be located? What will the hotel look like? What features and comforts will it offer?